MW00615066

BUILD YOUR *Child's*

MOUNTAIN

OF MONEY

INVESTING FOR
PARENTS AND TEENS

Save Early
Build Wealth With Dividend Stocks
Create Financial Freedom
Join FIRE-**SE**™

MIRIAM PAPKE   BILL PAPKE   ED ANDERSON

ISBN: 978-0-578-42297-8
eISBN: 978-0-578-42298-5

Editing courtesy of Jeanne Noorman
Stick Figures Courtesy of Andreas at *Shapechef.com*
Thank you, Jeanne and Andreas.

This Financial Journey

Belongs to

_____

To You, This Child I love
I want you to believe
Deep in your heart that
You are capable of achieving
Anything you put your mind to
That you will never lose

You either win or learn

I bless you to go forth
Thrive
Aim for the skies!
I can't promise to be here
For the rest of your life
But I can promise to love you
For the rest of mine.

Love,

Date

CONTENTS

Purpose of This Book

To help you build a **Mountain of Money** and create **Financial Freedom** for your children by the time they're in their 50's or much earlier, if you "ramp-up" your savings. The best strategy to build their **Mountain of Money** begins by starting early in their lives, buying dividend stocks and reinvesting all the dividends, or buying the S&P 500 Exchange Traded Fund (ETF) with the stock symbol SPY.

To record your child's financial journey. Plan to purchase one copy for each child and use this book to journal quarterly net-worth calculations. Beginning the process today will give you a legacy record of their trek toward **Financial Freedom.**

Ted's Investing Story

Before starting, we would like to tell you a story of how financial success is achieved when a person uses the investment guidelines outlined in this book.

Twenty years ago, a married friend with a six-month old child bought a new house that needed landscaping. Ted, a close friend in the landscaping business, did the work for $2000. Unbeknown to the home owners, the landscaper invested the $2000 in an account for the child. Upon graduation from high school, the teenager was presented with a surprise check for $9,800. This was the result of an 8% stock market return compounded for nearly 18 years.

In this book, we recommend that you open a stock investment account early, make regular deposits and reinvest dividends in the account. Then, when they're old enough to take the account over, encourage your child, teen, or young adult to continue adding to the account into their fifties. Ted's story doesn't show the teen picking up the investment task. But it does show that money grows, if invested according to these guidelines. We know that at some point after age 50, they will have taken big strides toward a goal of **Financial Freedom** and can choose to start spending the incoming dividends.

Forward

THIS BOOK IS FOR YOU IF:

- You want to build a financial legacy for a child you love who is between birth and age 17.

- You're a teenager with a goal to build wealth and gain **Financial Freedom.**

- You're an older person wishing to build your personal passive-income "stream".

- You want details and the first steps to building a legacy and teaching your child the principles of saving, investing, and financial security, beginning NOW.

GRANDPA'S GOALS

Work on interesting projects
Have a lot of fun
Make a lot of money

FINANCIAL FREEDOM is achieved when **income** from your investments equals your **spending**. You are then free to do whatever you want in life … including staying on your current path.

The four basic concepts to **Financial Freedom:**

1. Start early.
2. Spend less than you earn.
3. Use the savings to invest in the stock market.
4. Build the investments to create passive income through dividends.

Whether you're new to investing or an experienced veteran, we encourage you to follow the guidelines in this book, open a stock account, and get started. Your child may even thank you later in life!

We'll give you an explanation of financial terms and instructions to get your child started including:

- o Guidelines on how to save and invest at different stages and ages
- o Information on how to open a stock account
- o Instructions on how to invest in the stock account
- o Direction on tracking results using Net Worth

Disclaimer: There are many different philosophies on investing in the stock market. The one explained in this book is meant to be a steady, safe, reliable, long-term method that you can follow yourself and also teach your children. It is **not** meant to be a comprehensive exploration of the entire range of ways to invest in the stock market.

You will enjoy knowing the investment you're making in the future for this child will impact the lives of family members you may never meet as it has the potential to change the financial picture for generations to come.

Throughout this book you'll see notes with wisdom from Ed. You'll recognize them ~ They're labeled

EDvice.

Have fun!

Miriam, Bill, Ed

CHAPTER 1

Mountain of Money Magic Formula

Here's a sneak peek at where we're heading using a SAMPLE formula for reaching $1,000,000 by age 55!

1. Start with $7,500 which has been saved by age 15. (Gifts, starting at birth, and jobs, starting at age 10.)

2. Invest in dividend stocks as we suggest. The sample calculations below reflect 9.8% compound growth. (This is the AVERAGE growth of the stock market over the long haul.)

3. At age 15, Begin adding $60/month to your **Mountain of Money**.

4. Increase your monthly saving by 6% each year as you earn more money.

5. Surprise! Your **Mountain of Money** will have grown to:

SAMPLE MILESTONES:

AGE		
	15	$ 7,500
	30	$ 66,000
	40	$ 214,000
	50	$ 634,000
	55	$ 1,074,000

If you want to try it yourself, search online for 'Compound Interest Calculator' and play with different starting ages and dollar amounts!

What if I started LATER?

1. Start with $7,500 saved by age 30.

2. Invest in dividend stocks as we suggest. The SAMPLE calculations reflect 9.8% compound growth. (This is the AVERAGE growth of the stock market over the long haul.)

3. Begin adding $225/month to your **Mountain of Money**.

4. Increase your monthly saving by 6% each year as you earn more money.

5. Surprise! Your **Mountain of Money** will have grown to:

Mountain of Money Magic Formula

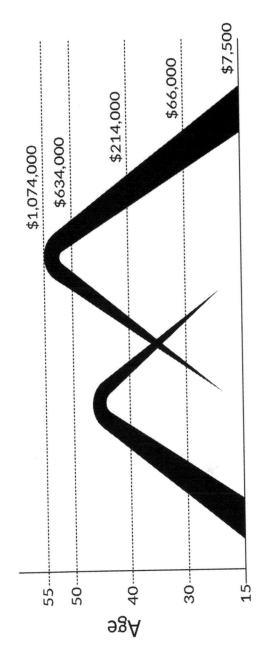

Mountain of Money Milestones

SAMPLE MILESTONES:

AGE		
30	$7,500
40	$ 77,000
50	$ 309,000
60	$ 1,007,000

EDvice

START NOW

Success is the accomplishment of a
predetermined goal

CHAPTER 2

What's in it for me?
I'm the "Facilitator"

Great question! You're investing time, love, and energy building a solid financial foundation for a child you love. There's no money in it for you – except that as you develop and teach this saving and investing habit, you may love seeing the dollars grow and decide to "save and invest" for yourself as well!

As facilitator, you will be a mentor, a coach, a cheerleader, and a financial guide. You're the one who:

- Models the 'save-to-invest' habit
- Sets the quarterly review appointments to monitor progress and set new goals
- Is responsible for transferring funds to the brokerage account for your child (I know it may sound complicated and scary, but we'll walk you through this process.)
- Ensures that the agreed-upon percentage of all gifts and earnings is set aside in the piggy bank or bank account (maybe adding spare change and a few dollars yourself as the mood strikes you.)
- AND you get bragging rights to your friends!

"Financial Independence, when used intelligently, can make you robust; it gives you options and allows you to make the right choices. Freedom is the ultimate option."

Talege Antifragile

CHAPTER 3

What's in it For Me?
I'm Just a Teenager

Financial Freedom at a young age. That's what's in it for you! You want to become successful, find a career you enjoy, and create your own life's journey. This takes time and, sometimes, a few course corrections.

Along the way, set the habit of saving and investing as we recommend in this book. By building a solid financial foundation, you will gain confidence in your future and have more choices when you get older.

Because you're starting NOW, your investing will provide the ability to live comfortably regardless of whether or not you have a high-paying job. The saving and long-term investing principals in this book work for any career.

Learning how to handle money will give you an advantage over your peers. **FINANCIAL FREEDOM** means you won't have to depend on other people. Building wealth will also give you the ability to invest in others by **GIVING GENEROUSLY**.

A goal without a plan is a wish.

Antoine de Saint-Exupéry

CHAPTER 4

Let's Explain a Few Terms

What does PRINCIPAL mean?

The amount of money you start with is called the "principal".

What's a STOCK?

Buying a share of stock means you own a small part of a large business.

What is INTEREST?

When depositing money in a bank account or purchasing a stock, you are loaning money to the company or bank. In return for this loan, they pay you a little money which is interest income from a bank and dividend income from a company.

What is a DIVIDEND?

The company you invest in pays you a small amount of money

for each share of stock you own. This payment is called a DIVIDEND. A dividend is essentially INTEREST earned on your stock investment. (That's why we're able to use a COMPOUND INTEREST tool to calculate growth.)

While some companies pay out monthly, most pay their dividends on a quarterly schedule (every 3 months). Choose to have your dividends automatically buy another partial share of the same stock. **Since 1950, over 40% of the gains in the stock market have been through dividends.**

One important concept with dividend stocks is that, for the most part, your dividends keep rolling into your account, regardless of the ups and downs of the overall stock market. You don't need to watch the short-term price changes in the underlying stocks. But if you do, you won't need to feel concerned. (We give "Sell Signal" guidelines in a later chapter.)

What is FINANCIAL FREEDOM?

It's the point at which your annual income from your investments equals or exceeds your annual spending.

What is PASSIVE INCOME?

Passive income is income you collect separately from an earned paycheck. It comes rolling in when you're sleeping or at the beach. We like that!

One great way to receive passive income is to save money and invest in stocks that pay dividends. The money you save goes to work for you in the stock market and earns more money.

Disclaimer: There are a wide array of ways to generate passive income. We've chosen investing in dividend stocks because the entry level investment is low, and it is something you can set up and let grow for a lifetime.

What is the COMPOUNDING Effect?

This is the process where dividends are earned and then added to the principal amount. Over time, the principal grows as dividends are added to it. Then, you earn money on the bigger pile of money (increased principal)! It's building your **MOUNTAIN OF MONEY** and it's a good deal!

When money is invested carefully, it grows each year. The dividend amount that is added to the principal is determined by the dividend rate.

In a sample Compounding Effect calculation, $1000 invested at 10% is worth $1100 at the end of year 1. ($1000 x 1.10) = $1100.

The amount at the beginning of year 2 (the principal) will be $1100 as calculated above. If this is invested again at 10%, the value at the end of year 2 will be ($1100 x 1.10) = $1210

A Compounding Effect calculation keeps adding the yearly dividends to the principal. This means you begin to earn "INTEREST on the INTEREST". Over time, the principal growth begins to accelerate, and with it, the annual income grows moving you toward the goal of **Financial Freedom.**

Here's an example graph showing how an initial investment of $1000, with just $50/month added, and invested on the stock market compounding at an average of 9.8%, annually can be worth over $221,000 in 35 years. Of that total amount, just $22,000 was money you invested (the Principal), and the rest was earned income.

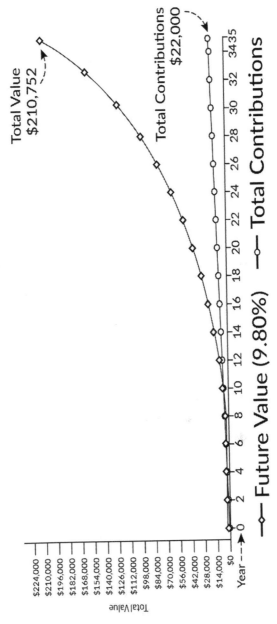

What is the S&P 500?

This is a formula for tracking the OVERALL PERFOR-MANCE of the stock market. 500 large companies make up the S&P 500 Index listing.

The S&P 500 Index has grown an *average* of 9.8% per year over the last 90 years.

What is the 200-DAY MOVING AVERAGE?

The average closing price of a stock or the S&P Index over the last 200 days. This is a trend line showing the general direction that a stock (or the overall stock market) has gone over the last 200 days.

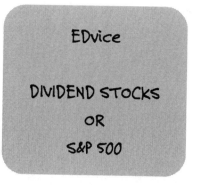

EDvice

DIVIDEND STOCKS
OR
S&P 500

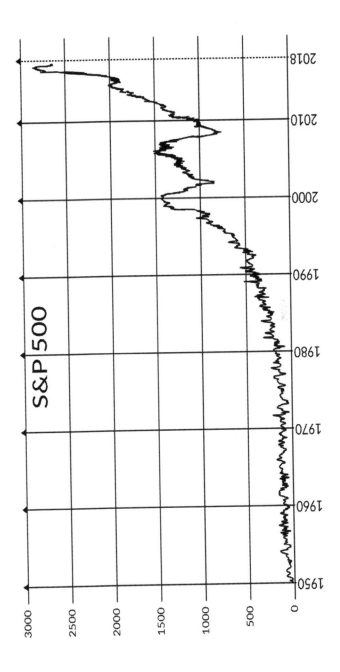

CHAPTER 5

Two Dividend Investing Strategies

Here are two strategies for investing in stocks. They both take advantage of dividends.

The FIRST concept is to purchase **individual stocks** that pay dividends. Then, those dividends are reinvested to purchase more dividend-paying stocks.

If you choose to invest in individual stocks, you can begin by searching a pre-selected list. DIVIDEND ARISTOCRATS is a great place to start. This is a select group of 50+/- S&P 500 stocks with 25+ years of consecutive dividend increases. Since

1991, the DIVIDEND ARISTOCRATS group has achieved an average annual return of 12.9%.

One possible strategy is selecting 10-12 of the highest yielding stocks from the DIVIDEND ARISTOCRATS list. If you choose from this carefully selected list, you won't need to research the other thousands of dividend-paying stocks. The list is updated annually, so you may want to check back with the list from time to time. An excellent dividend stock reference website is *DividendInvestor.com*

The SECOND concept is to buy a stock that follows the **overall performance** of the stock market. This is an Exchange Traded Fund (ETF) with the stock symbol SPY. SPY contains all of the S&P 500 stocks and its growth includes gains from dividends.

The advantage of this second concept is that it's easy – you don't have to determine which individual dividend-paying stocks to purchase. In effect, you are on "autopilot"! Just buy more SPY with your new cash.

A possible disadvantage: This S&P 500 strategy doesn't create a lot of excitement for your young investor (if that's one of your goals).

CHAPTER 6

Financial Freedom Graph

The **FINANCIAL FREEDOM GRAPH** explains the principle of growing your passive income to equal your spending (or the spending level you wish to have for yourself and your family). Once you get there, you are financially free and can choose the way you want to spend your time. Do you want to continue working full or part time? Do you want to spend more time with people you love, volunteer, or explore a new hobby?

Financial Freedom: this is the milestone in your life when your "passive" income equals or exceeds your spending. In other words, you aren't required to continue

working to maintain your chosen lifestyle. The point at which this milestone is achieved depends solely on your decisions – on the amount you earn, save, gift, and invest, as well as when you start.

The Graph consists of 5 lines:

The **EARNINGS INCOME** line indicates the money that you earn from your job. It begins very slowly with part-time work in your teens, then accelerates quickly as you obtain your first full-time employment. Your income grows over time as you get increases in pay and move to better jobs along your career path. At some point in your life, you are able to reduce your work hours (because you have grown your PASSIVE IN-COME line) so your earnings income goes down.

The **SPENDING** line indicates how much money you spend every year. As your needs increase, your family grows, and you earn more money, your spending line goes up. At some point, your spending may flatten or decrease because you have paid for major things like your home or investments for your children's education. Note that the spending line must be below the earnings income line in order to accumulate savings.

The **ACCUMULATED SAVINGS** line indicates how much money you have saved by spending less than you earned. This line is the amount of money you have available to invest in the stock market to obtain passive income thru dividends. By investing, you are building a **Mountain of Money**, which is growing more money.

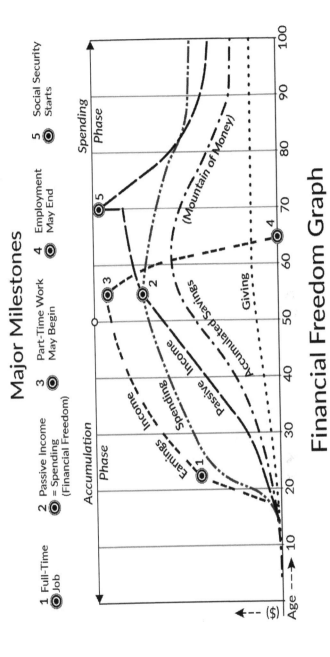

Financial Freedom Graph

Major Milestones

1 ⊚ Full-Time Job

2 ⊚ Passive Income = Spending (Financial Freedom)

3 ⊚ Part-Time Work May Begin

4 ⊚ Employment May End

5 ⊚ Social Security Starts

Spending Phase

Accumulation Phase

(Mountain of Money)

Accumulated Savings

Giving

Passive Income

Spending

Earnings Income

($)

Age

The **PASSIVE INCOME** line indicates how much money is coming in from your invested stocks that pay dividends. The money that comes in is re-invested, not spent. Then, through the power of the COMPOUNDING EFFECT, it begins to grow very rapidly as time passes. DO NOT begin to consume the passive income until it equals your annual spending.

If you have invested primarily in the Exchange Traded Fund (ETF) with the stock symbol SPY, the time to convert that investment into individual dividend-paying stocks is when your annual passive income equals your annual spending. (Milestone 2 on the FINANCIAL FREEDOM GRAPH) Your goal is to select at least a dozen different stocks to reduce your risk and obtain a blend of different dividend rates and start the flow of your passive income stream.

The **GIVING** line shows a commitment to INVESTING IN OTHERS by setting aside a portion of your income for causes you support. This line grows as your income grows.

Notice that the Graph has an "accumulation" phase, up to the point of the **Financial Freedom** milestone followed by a "spending/philanthropic (giving away)" phase. At some point, you begin to withdraw or spend the accumulated savings, leaving some of it to others as an inheritance.

CHAPTER 7

Giving and Receiving

Here's an important concept: EVERYTHING we have, has been given to us by God, the Creator of the universe. If you think in those terms, giving back becomes an important part of the financial equation.

So, there are three things you need to do with the money that you earn:

1: SAVE
2: SPEND
3: GIVE

SAVING

Saving is setting aside money for future use rather than spending everything you earn. Saving is essentially INVESTING IN YOURSELF. This book is about what to do with the money you save: Investing in the Stock Market by buying Dividend Stocks or investing in the Stock Market by buying Index Funds with the stock symbol (SPY) that simply follow the growth of the overall market.

You may want to adjust these guidelines based upon your age and income. The most important concept about saving is: START NOW and use the power of the COMPOUNDING EFFECT and time to make your money grow for you.

SPENDING

Spending is obvious – it's what you need for your everyday life, food, clothing, shelter. You determine your lifestyle by your spending priorities. If you pay out all that you earn, there will be nothing to save or invest for the future and nothing left to give.

So, the big idea is to SPEND LESS than you earn. In order to do this, you create a BUDGET that allows you to set goals for various spending categories. Each person's budget will be unique to their needs and wishes. Creating the budget is only the first step; tracking and adjusting the budget on a regular basis is the second step. We suggest you evaluate and adjust your budget at least once per year.

Using a debit card allows you to spend only what you have in your bank account and is a wiser choice than using a credit card, which allows you to borrow money automatically. Avoid credit (borrowing money) except for big purchases like a home. Stay out of debt by using cash, checks, or a debit card.

GIVING

Giving back is essentially INVESTING IN OTHERS. You choose to use a portion of your resources to help someone else. Think of all the things you have received – the love of your parents, a home, an education, the list is endless.

The Bible's guideline for giving 10% of what you earn is known as a tithe. This should be part of your budget. When you give, you receive back many times over.

DO IT NOW

Have you decided on an investing strategy?

The choices:

- S&P 500 (SPY)* investments
- Individual Dividend stocks

If you need to re-read the section explaining the difference between the two, please do it now.

*Remember, if you start with the S&P 500 you'll need to move to individual dividend stocks later to generate interest income and create a passive income stream.

CHAPTER 8

Let's Get Started

First: Collect financial information (Net Worth) and hunt-down any cash the child has. You'll need to gather savings account balances, coin collection totals, and the balances of investment accounts other people may have already established. You'll also need the child's Social Security number.

Second: Look at the NET WORTH calculation on page 35. Familiarize yourself with the format and make sure you have the financial information needed to complete the first one. This may be a bit cumbersome the first couple of times, but after that, you'll be a pro. You can help the child pick up this task at some point early on.

Third: Set a time to connect with your child (or children). This can be a great conversation for several children in one family. However, if the ages are widely spread, plan separate connection times.

CHAPTER 9

Child's Age Guidelines

- BIRTH to 3 YEARS - Facilitator saves to invest 50% of all gift money and income.

- 3 to 5 YEARS - Facilitator invests 50%. Teaches coin values.

- 5 to 9 YEARS - Facilitator invests 50%. Begins paying an allowance or paying for chores completed. Explains Stock dividends and bank interest. (The child is loaning or sharing money with the company or bank. They're being paid a little money [interest/dividend] for sharing.)

- 9 to 13 YEARS - Facilitator invests 50%. Explains the process to the child: 50% savings of all gifts and income, 10% charitable giving, balance for gifts and stuff they want.

- 13 to 15 YEARS - Facilitator and child invest. Encourage the child to become involved in determining account value and recording their new Net Worth. Drop the save to invest percentage from 50% savings to 25%. Encourage the child to find a part-time job.
- 15 - 18 YEARS Facilitator and child invest. Increase the allowance or adjust the family chore responsibilities and the amount paid per chore.

CHAPTER 10

Now Connect and DO IT

Set a Time

Meet with your child, beginning as early as age 3. Making this a special "together" time, which means you will both look forward to it – maybe going out for ice cream or to eat together. Bring this book and the financial details you've collected to the meeting.

Calculate Net Worth

Net Worth is CASH minus LIABILITIES.

CASH is … Cash or anything owned outright that can be converted to cash.

LIABILITIES are cash or cash equivalents that you owe to a person or to an institution.

Good for you! You're connecting a young person to the awareness that money is important and that understanding and building a healthy, growing passive income stream is a wise financial choice.

You'll find many years of Net Worth recording pages at the end of the book. Plan to connect with each child, calculate and record their Net Worth every three months for years to come. Tracking the Net Worth calculation over years will give the child a graphic picture of the power of saving to invest early and compounding interest.

NET WORTH CALCULATION

ASSETS   DATE _____

    1. Cash on hand   _____

    2. Cash: Savings   _____

    3. Cash: Money Market   _____

    4. Credit Union Funds   _____

    5. Bonds   _____

    6. Stock   _____

    7. Valuable Coins   _____

    8. Other   _____

Total Assets   _____

Liabilities

    1.   _____

    2.   _____

Total Liabilities   _____

Net Worth: Assets – Liabilities   _____

Next quarterly meeting date: _____

NOTES:

CHAPTER 11

13 Easy Steps to Opening a Stock Account

1. Open a TD Ameritrade custodial account in the child's name. (You'll need the child's social security number). Any discount broker can be used, but TD Ameritrade is user friendly and customer service oriented. Feel free to call and have a customer service representative walk you through the first few transactions.

2. Note the Account user name and password and store them in a safe place.

3. Select the REINVEST DIVIDENDS tab.

4. Once $200 cash has been saved from the Net Worth calculation, fund the TD Ameritrade account and begin investing. (Do not purchase a stock with less than $200, as there is a $5.95 charge per transaction for both purchases and sales.)

5. Make or buy a piggy bank for the child's room.

6. Place 50% of any gift money the child gets into the piggy bank. (You can add change or dollar bills once in a while, if you like.)

7. Each time the child's bank has accumulated $100, transfer it to TD Ameritrade.

8. Each time the TD Ameritrade account reaches $200, purchase a currently owned stock until you own $750 worth of that particular stock. Then, buy a new stock or more SPY.

9. Calculate and record the starting Net Worth, then recalculate on January 1, April 1, July 1 and October 1 each year.

10. Recording the increase in the Net Worth pages is very important. The child and you will begin to appreciate the power of compounding interest.

11. Discuss with the child the resulting change in their Net Worth at each quarterly calculation. Start this around age 3 or 4. Who knows at what age the child will begin to understand some part of the discussion?

12. As their income increases, let them help pick new stock purchases.

13. Once they become employed, strongly encourage them to open a Roth IRA stock account. This investing vehicle will allow them to withdraw earnings tax free, after age 59 1/2.

Many stocks pay monthly dividends. You'll see monthly progress quickly if you purchase monthly dividend payers for the first 4 or 5 stocks. Until the Net Worth grows, limit any investment in a single stock to $750. This will spread the risk by not putting all your eggs in the same basket.

Additional suggested reading:
10 RULES OF SAFE INVESTING by Harry Brown.

CHAPTER 12

Long Term Strategy

The investing concept in this book is a LONG-TERM STRATEGY. This means you buy and hold stocks, rather than trade in and out frequently. As the chart of the performance of the S&P 500 showed, there are *significant ups and downs* from year to year. But you can see that the **long-term trend line is UP**. Investing in dividend paying stocks means that the dividends generally keep coming, even in down years.

Although the **overall average** increase in the stock market over the past 90 years has been 9.8%, there have been years (and decades) with significant losses. This is known as a market "correction" or a "bear" market. One thing is for certain: nobody can predict the future. So, your strategy should remain the same in good times and in bad.

CHAPTER 13

Should You Ever Sell? — YES

SELL SIGNAL

You've been advised throughout this book to buy dividend stocks and reinvest the dividends or buy the S&P 500 ETF with the stock symbol SPY and hold it to build a **Mountain of Money**. If your child's account is started at an early age, there will be one or more bear market *setbacks* on their road to age 50 to 55. To avoid a big financial loss on this climb, consider the following and act 100% of the time without question.

If the price of any of your stocks drops 8% percent or more *below* the 200-day moving average, SELL the stock. BUY the stock back when it has closed 8% *above* the 200-day moving average. You will already have a loss, but you will avoid an upcoming larger loss.

CHAPTER 14

You've Built Your Mountain of Money

GREAT! You've reached **Financial Freedom**! Now, it's time to live off the dividend income and reduce or eliminate your employment making any lifestyle adjustments you wish to make.

You can travel, start a new hobby, spend more time with family, whatever you dream of doing next. Now, rather than reinvesting your dividends, it's time to have them deposited directly into your bank account.

At age 55, you can also begin withdrawing a small percentage from your principal amount (**Mountain of Money**) *and* spending the dividends.

If you've invested in a Roth IRA, your income from the Roth account will be tax free, if withdrawn after age 59 ½.

Let's say your **Mountain of Money** is $1,000,000. A 4% dividend rate, plus a 2% withdrawal rate will generate a $60,000 annual income. At this point, your lifestyle and giving choices will determine your actions.

CHAPTER 15

Final Note to Teens

....What Should You Do?

What is a "job"? Is it work, fun, or a method to make money? The ideal career is one that allows you to follow your interest, your so-called "passion", to do something you like (not something that someone else has dictated to you). In that sense, your job should not seem like "work". Getting up each day and looking forward to a career opportunity is an ideal goal to achieve.

Sure, your initial job (washing dishes, digging ditches or cutting grass) might not be ideal, but it's a first step which leads to your bigger goal of a productive life and financial freedom. I (Bill) started by mowing lawns (Bill's Lawn Service), washing dishes and clearing tables at a restaurant, behind the counter at McDonalds, and sweeping floors in a cookie factory. I didn't dislike any of those jobs, partly because I knew they were temporary tools to get me a career as an architect.

The second, and equally important criteria of a job is your skillset. That is, what are you good at? What is your special capability, your "talent"? Your particular skill might be writing, drawing, speaking, playing a sport or musical instrument, teaching, solving problems…the list goes on. So, a critical part of life is finding out what your passions and skills are. Your ideal job is one that finds the *intersection of y*our passions and skills. You need both. It does no good to be passionate about golf but have no skill in playing the game, no matter how much you practice.

So, how do you discover this intersection of "passion" and "skill"? Part of the discovery process is trial and error. You just have to try things out. Initially, your parents enrolled you in certain things in school, such as sports, band, etc. Now it's your turn to try things on your own and follow your gut.

About the Authors

Thank you for inviting us into your family financial discussion. We each learned lessons on our life-treks that led us to a very real awareness of the need to understand and direct our personal financial futures. We share a few of the lessons here, hoping that you'll use them to build a strong, self-directed financial path and avoid some of the learning curves we experienced. Enjoy the lessons, talk with your family, and grow your relationships as you grow your child's **Mountain of Money**.

MIRIAM'S STORY

My grandpa gifted me with shares of IBM stock when I was born. It was good to receive a quarterly dividend check to spend, have money to fully fund my college education, and have funds to take care of a few big financial obligations early in my adult life. Notice the trend here... the words "spend", "fully fund", and "take care of financial obligations" all mean the money was going OUT. I had a golden ticket. Not understanding the investing process or the value of what was given to me, I casually let it slip away. This book will remedy that! You will KNOW how to build a healthy financial foundation that will give your child (and maybe you!) life choices few other folks enjoy including freedom from financial worry later in life.

Miriam Papke

BILL'S STORY

Investing first caught my attention in a high school class segment that introduced me to the stock market. The class project was to pick a stock, pretend we owned it, and then follow it for a semester. My pick, Brunswick (the bowling equipment manufacturer) took off upward, and I was "hooked". My parents taught me to save using a bank savings account but not how to invest. The initial purpose of saving was to afford a college education to become an architect. It wasn't until after I got my first full-time job that I became aware of the idea of passive income (after reading numerous books on investing).

This led to my opening a traditional stock account and then self-directed investing thru TD Ameritrade accounts such as IRAs and other retirement accounts. I was able to achieve **Financial Freedom** in my 50's through a combination of stock accounts and successful real estate ventures.

Bill Papke

ED'S STORY

My investing in stocks started at age 60 after an early and unplanned retirement. Each time I calculated my retirement income in the years leading up to age 65, the end value was equal to my salary. I did not save to bolster my retirement income. My parents did not discuss saving or investing money. I did not discuss saving or investing money with my two sons. Now, I am very aware of the need to provide investing guidance to my two sons, eleven grandchildren, and nine great grandchildren and get them started on the road to **Financial Freedom**. We have co-authored this book with step-by-step instructions on a method to achieve this goal.

Ed Anderson (aka EDvice)

ASSETS   DATE _____

    1. Cash on hand   _____

    2. Cash: Savings   _____

    3. Cash: Money Market   _____

    4. Credit Union Funds   _____

    5. Bonds   _____

    6. Stock   _____

    7. Valuable Coins   _____

    8. Other   _____

Total Assets   _____

Liabilities

    1.   _____

    2.   _____

Total Liabilities   _____

Net Worth: Assets – Liabilities   _____

Next quarterly meeting date: _____

NOTES:

ASSETS   DATE _____

    1. Cash on hand   _____

    2. Cash: Savings   _____

    3. Cash: Money Market   _____

    4. Credit Union Funds   _____

    5. Bonds   _____

    6. Stock   _____

    7. Valuable Coins   _____

    8. Other   _____

Total Assets   _____

Liabilities

    1.   _____

    2.   _____

Total Liabilities   _____

Net Worth: Assets – Liabilities   _____

Next quarterly meeting date: _____

NOTES:

ASSETS   DATE _____

    1. Cash on hand   _____

    2. Cash: Savings   _____

    3. Cash: Money Market   _____

    4. Credit Union Funds   _____

    5. Bonds   _____

    6. Stock   _____

    7. Valuable Coins   _____

    8. Other   _____

Total Assets   _____

Liabilities

    1.   _____

    2.   _____

Total Liabilities   _____

Net Worth: Assets – Liabilities   _____

Next quarterly meeting date: _____

NOTES:

ASSETS   DATE _____

    1. Cash on hand   _____

    2. Cash: Savings   _____

    3. Cash: Money Market   _____

    4. Credit Union Funds   _____

    5. Bonds   _____

    6. Stock   _____

    7. Valuable Coins   _____

    8. Other   _____

Total Assets   _____

Liabilities

    1.   _____

    2.   _____

Total Liabilities   _____

Net Worth: Assets – Liabilities   _____

Next quarterly meeting date: _____

NOTES:

ASSETS   DATE _____

    1. Cash on hand   _____

    2. Cash: Savings   _____

    3. Cash: Money Market   _____

    4. Credit Union Funds   _____

    5. Bonds   _____

    6. Stock   _____

    7. Valuable Coins   _____

    8. Other   _____

Total Assets   _____

Liabilities

    1.   _____

    2.   _____

Total Liabilities   _____

Net Worth: Assets – Liabilities   _____

Next quarterly meeting date: _____

NOTES:

ASSETS   DATE _____

    1. Cash on hand   _____

    2. Cash: Savings   _____

    3. Cash: Money Market   _____

    4. Credit Union Funds   _____

    5. Bonds   _____

    6. Stock   _____

    7. Valuable Coins   _____

    8. Other   _____

Total Assets   _____

Liabilities

    1.   _____

    2.   _____

Total Liabilities   _____

Net Worth: Assets – Liabilities   _____

Next quarterly meeting date: _____

NOTES:

ASSETS   DATE _____

    1. Cash on hand   _____

    2. Cash: Savings   _____

    3. Cash: Money Market   _____

    4. Credit Union Funds   _____

    5. Bonds   _____

    6. Stock   _____

    7. Valuable Coins   _____

    8. Other   _____

Total Assets   _____

Liabilities

    1.   _____

    2.   _____

Total Liabilities   _____

Net Worth: Assets – Liabilities   _____

Next quarterly meeting date: _____

NOTES:

ASSETS   DATE _____

    1. Cash on hand   _____

    2. Cash: Savings   _____

    3. Cash: Money Market   _____

    4. Credit Union Funds   _____

    5. Bonds   _____

    6. Stock   _____

    7. Valuable Coins   _____

    8. Other   _____

Total Assets   _____

Liabilities

    1.   _____

    2.   _____

Total Liabilities   _____

Net Worth: Assets – Liabilities   _____

Next quarterly meeting date: _____

NOTES:

ASSETS   DATE _____

    1. Cash on hand   _____

    2. Cash: Savings   _____

    3. Cash: Money Market   _____

    4. Credit Union Funds   _____

    5. Bonds   _____

    6. Stock   _____

    7. Valuable Coins   _____

    8. Other   _____

Total Assets   _____

Liabilities

    1.   _____

    2.   _____

Total Liabilities   _____

Net Worth: Assets – Liabilities   _____

Next quarterly meeting date: _____

NOTES:

ASSETS   DATE _____

    1. Cash on hand   _____

    2. Cash: Savings   _____

    3. Cash: Money Market   _____

    4. Credit Union Funds   _____

    5. Bonds   _____

    6. Stock   _____

    7. Valuable Coins   _____

    8. Other   _____

Total Assets   _____

Liabilities

    1.   _____

    2.   _____

Total Liabilities   _____

Net Worth: Assets – Liabilities   _____

Next quarterly meeting date: _____

NOTES:

ASSETS   DATE _____

    1. Cash on hand   _____

    2. Cash: Savings   _____

    3. Cash: Money Market   _____

    4. Credit Union Funds   _____

    5. Bonds   _____

    6. Stock   _____

    7. Valuable Coins   _____

    8. Other   _____

Total Assets   _____

Liabilities

    1.   _____

    2.   _____

Total Liabilities   _____

Net Worth: Assets – Liabilities   _____

Next quarterly meeting date: _____

NOTES:

ASSETS   DATE _____

    1. Cash on hand   _____

    2. Cash: Savings   _____

    3. Cash: Money Market   _____

    4. Credit Union Funds   _____

    5. Bonds   _____

    6. Stock   _____

    7. Valuable Coins   _____

    8. Other   _____

Total Assets   _____

Liabilities

    1.   _____

    2.   _____

Total Liabilities   _____

Net Worth: Assets – Liabilities   _____

Next quarterly meeting date: _____

NOTES:

ASSETS   DATE _____

    1. Cash on hand   _____

    2. Cash: Savings   _____

    3. Cash: Money Market   _____

    4. Credit Union Funds   _____

    5. Bonds   _____

    6. Stock   _____

    7. Valuable Coins   _____

    8. Other   _____

Total Assets   _____

Liabilities

    1.   _____

    2.   _____

Total Liabilities   _____

Net Worth: Assets – Liabilities   _____

Next quarterly meeting date: _____

NOTES:

ASSETS   DATE _____

    1. Cash on hand   _____

    2. Cash: Savings   _____

    3. Cash: Money Market   _____

    4. Credit Union Funds   _____

    5. Bonds   _____

    6. Stock   _____

    7. Valuable Coins   _____

    8. Other   _____

Total Assets   _____

Liabilities

    1.   _____

    2.   _____

Total Liabilities   _____

Net Worth: Assets – Liabilities   _____

Next quarterly meeting date: _____

NOTES:

ASSETS   DATE _____

    1. Cash on hand   _____

    2. Cash: Savings   _____

    3. Cash: Money Market   _____

    4. Credit Union Funds   _____

    5. Bonds   _____

    6. Stock   _____

    7. Valuable Coins   _____

    8. Other   _____

Total Assets   _____

Liabilities

    1.   _____

    2.   _____

Total Liabilities   _____

Net Worth: Assets – Liabilities   _____

Next quarterly meeting date: _____

NOTES:

ASSETS   DATE _____

    1. Cash on hand   _____

    2. Cash: Savings   _____

    3. Cash: Money Market   _____

    4. Credit Union Funds   _____

    5. Bonds   _____

    6. Stock   _____

    7. Valuable Coins   _____

    8. Other   _____

Total Assets   _____

Liabilities

    1.   _____

    2.   _____

Total Liabilities   _____

Net Worth: Assets – Liabilities   _____

Next quarterly meeting date: _____

NOTES:

ASSETS   DATE _____

    1. Cash on hand   _____

    2. Cash: Savings   _____

    3. Cash: Money Market   _____

    4. Credit Union Funds   _____

    5. Bonds   _____

    6. Stock   _____

    7. Valuable Coins   _____

    8. Other   _____

Total Assets   _____

Liabilities

    1.   _____

    2.   _____

Total Liabilities   _____

Net Worth: Assets – Liabilities   _____

Next quarterly meeting date: _____

NOTES:

ASSETS   DATE _____

    1. Cash on hand   _____

    2. Cash: Savings   _____

    3. Cash: Money Market   _____

    4. Credit Union Funds   _____

    5. Bonds   _____

    6. Stock   _____

    7. Valuable Coins   _____

    8. Other   _____

Total Assets   _____

Liabilities

    1.   _____

    2.   _____

Total Liabilities   _____

Net Worth: Assets – Liabilities   _____

Next quarterly meeting date: _____

NOTES:

ASSETS   DATE _____

    1. Cash on hand   _____

    2. Cash: Savings   _____

    3. Cash: Money Market   _____

    4. Credit Union Funds   _____

    5. Bonds   _____

    6. Stock   _____

    7. Valuable Coins   _____

    8. Other   _____

Total Assets   _____

Liabilities

    1.   _____

    2.   _____

Total Liabilities   _____

Net Worth: Assets – Liabilities   _____

Next quarterly meeting date: _____

NOTES:

ASSETS   DATE _____

    1. Cash on hand   _____

    2. Cash: Savings   _____

    3. Cash: Money Market   _____

    4. Credit Union Funds   _____

    5. Bonds   _____

    6. Stock   _____

    7. Valuable Coins   _____

    8. Other   _____

Total Assets   _____

Liabilities

    1.   _____

    2.   _____

Total Liabilities   _____

Net Worth: Assets – Liabilities   _____

Next quarterly meeting date: _____

NOTES:

ASSETS   DATE _____

    1. Cash on hand   _____

    2. Cash: Savings   _____

    3. Cash: Money Market   _____

    4. Credit Union Funds   _____

    5. Bonds   _____

    6. Stock   _____

    7. Valuable Coins   _____

    8. Other   _____

Total Assets   _____

Liabilities

    1.   _____

    2.   _____

Total Liabilities   _____

Net Worth: Assets – Liabilities   _____

Next quarterly meeting date: _____

NOTES:

ASSETS   DATE _____

    1. Cash on hand   _____

    2. Cash: Savings   _____

    3. Cash: Money Market   _____

    4. Credit Union Funds   _____

    5. Bonds   _____

    6. Stock   _____

    7. Valuable Coins   _____

    8. Other   _____

Total Assets   _____

Liabilities

    1.

    2.   _____

Total Liabilities   _____
                                  _____

Net Worth: Assets – Liabilities   _____

Next quarterly meeting date: _____

NOTES:

ASSETS   DATE _____

    1. Cash on hand   _____

    2. Cash: Savings   _____

    3. Cash: Money Market   _____

    4. Credit Union Funds   _____

    5. Bonds   _____

    6. Stock   _____

    7. Valuable Coins   _____

    8. Other   _____

Total Assets   _____

Liabilities

    1.   _____

    2.   _____

Total Liabilities   _____

Net Worth: Assets – Liabilities   _____

Next quarterly meeting date: _____

NOTES:

ASSETS

DATE _____

    1. Cash on hand

    _____

    2. Cash: Savings

    _____

    3. Cash: Money Market

    _____

    4. Credit Union Funds

    _____

    5. Bonds

    _____

    6. Stock

    _____

    7. Valuable Coins

    _____

    8. Other

    _____

Total Assets

_____

Liabilities

    1.

    _____

    2.

    _____

Total Liabilities

_____

Net Worth: Assets – Liabilities

_____

Next quarterly meeting date:

_____

NOTES:

ASSETS   DATE _____

    1. Cash on hand   _____

    2. Cash: Savings   _____

    3. Cash: Money Market   _____

    4. Credit Union Funds   _____

    5. Bonds   _____

    6. Stock   _____

    7. Valuable Coins   _____

    8. Other   _____

Total Assets   _____

Liabilities

    1.   _____

    2.   _____

Total Liabilities   _____

Net Worth: Assets – Liabilities   _____

Next quarterly meeting date: _____

NOTES:

ASSETS   DATE _____

    1. Cash on hand   _____

    2. Cash: Savings   _____

    3. Cash: Money Market   _____

    4. Credit Union Funds   _____

    5. Bonds   _____

    6. Stock   _____

    7. Valuable Coins   _____

    8. Other   _____

Total Assets   _____

Liabilities

    1.   _____

    2.   _____

Total Liabilities   _____

Net Worth: Assets – Liabilities   _____

Next quarterly meeting date: _____

NOTES:

ASSETS   DATE _____

    1. Cash on hand   _____

    2. Cash: Savings   _____

    3. Cash: Money Market   _____

    4. Credit Union Funds   _____

    5. Bonds   _____

    6. Stock   _____

    7. Valuable Coins   _____

    8. Other   _____

Total Assets   _____

Liabilities

    1.   _____

    2.   _____

Total Liabilities   _____

Net Worth: Assets – Liabilities   _____

Next quarterly meeting date: _____

NOTES:

ASSETS

DATE _____

    1. Cash on hand   _____

    2. Cash: Savings   _____

    3. Cash: Money Market _____

    4. Credit Union Funds   _____

    5. Bonds   _____

    6. Stock   _____

    7. Valuable Coins   _____

    8. Other   _____

Total Assets   _____

Liabilities

    1.   _____

    2.   _____

Total Liabilities   _____

Net Worth: Assets – Liabilities   _____

Next quarterly meeting date: _____

NOTES:

ASSETS   DATE _____

    1. Cash on hand   _____

    2. Cash: Savings   _____

    3. Cash: Money Market   _____

    4. Credit Union Funds   _____

    5. Bonds   _____

    6. Stock   _____

    7. Valuable Coins   _____

    8. Other   _____

Total Assets   _____

Liabilities

    1.   _____

    2.   _____

Total Liabilities   _____

Net Worth: Assets – Liabilities   _____

Next quarterly meeting date: _____

NOTES:

ASSETS   DATE _____

    1. Cash on hand   _____

    2. Cash: Savings   _____

    3. Cash: Money Market   _____

    4. Credit Union Funds   _____

    5. Bonds   _____

    6. Stock   _____

    7. Valuable Coins   _____

    8. Other   _____

Total Assets   _____

Liabilities

    1.   _____

    2.   _____

Total Liabilities   _____

Net Worth: Assets – Liabilities   _____

Next quarterly meeting date: _____

NOTES:

ASSETS   DATE _____

    1. Cash on hand   _____

    2. Cash: Savings   _____

    3. Cash: Money Market   _____

    4. Credit Union Funds   _____

    5. Bonds   _____

    6. Stock   _____

    7. Valuable Coins   _____

    8. Other   _____

Total Assets   _____

Liabilities

    1.   _____

    2.   _____

Total Liabilities   _____

Net Worth: Assets – Liabilities   _____

Next quarterly meeting date: _____

NOTES:

ASSETS   DATE _____

    1. Cash on hand   _____

    2. Cash: Savings   _____

    3. Cash: Money Market   _____

    4. Credit Union Funds   _____

    5. Bonds   _____

    6. Stock   _____

    7. Valuable Coins   _____

    8. Other   _____

Total Assets   _____

Liabilities

    1.

    2.   _____

Total Liabilities   _____

Net Worth: Assets – Liabilities   _____

Next quarterly meeting date: _____

NOTES:

ASSETS   DATE _____

    1. Cash on hand   _____

    2. Cash: Savings   _____

    3. Cash: Money Market   _____

    4. Credit Union Funds   _____

    5. Bonds   _____

    6. Stock   _____

    7. Valuable Coins   _____

    8. Other   _____

Total Assets   _____

Liabilities

    1.   _____

    2.   _____

Total Liabilities   _____

Net Worth: Assets – Liabilities   _____

Next quarterly meeting date: _____

NOTES:

ASSETS   DATE _____

    1. Cash on hand   _____

    2. Cash: Savings   _____

    3. Cash: Money Market   _____

    4. Credit Union Funds   _____

    5. Bonds   _____

    6. Stock   _____

    7. Valuable Coins   _____

    8. Other   _____

Total Assets   _____

Liabilities

    1.   _____

    2.   _____

Total Liabilities   _____

Net Worth: Assets − Liabilities   _____

Next quarterly meeting date: _____

NOTES:

ASSETS   DATE _____

    1. Cash on hand   _____

    2. Cash: Savings   _____

    3. Cash: Money Market   _____

    4. Credit Union Funds   _____

    5. Bonds   _____

    6. Stock   _____

    7. Valuable Coins   _____

    8. Other   _____

Total Assets   _____

Liabilities

    1.   _____

    2.   _____

Total Liabilities   _____

Net Worth: Assets – Liabilities   _____

Next quarterly meeting date: _____

NOTES:

ASSETS   DATE _____

    1. Cash on hand   _____

    2. Cash: Savings   _____

    3. Cash: Money Market   _____

    4. Credit Union Funds   _____

    5. Bonds   _____

    6. Stock   _____

    7. Valuable Coins   _____

    8. Other   _____

Total Assets   _____

Liabilities

    1.   _____

    2.   _____

Total Liabilities   _____

Net Worth: Assets – Liabilities   _____

Next quarterly meeting date: _____

NOTES:

ASSETS   DATE _____

    1. Cash on hand   _____

    2. Cash: Savings   _____

    3. Cash: Money Market   _____

    4. Credit Union Funds   _____

    5. Bonds   _____

    6. Stock   _____

    7. Valuable Coins   _____

    8. Other   _____

Total Assets   _____

Liabilities

    1.   _____

    2.   _____

Total Liabilities   _____

Net Worth: Assets – Liabilities   _____

Next quarterly meeting date: _____

NOTES:

ASSETS   DATE _____

    1. Cash on hand   _____

    2. Cash: Savings   _____

    3. Cash: Money Market   _____

    4. Credit Union Funds   _____

    5. Bonds   _____

    6. Stock   _____

    7. Valuable Coins   _____

    8. Other   _____

Total Assets   _____

Liabilities

    1.   _____

    2.   _____

Total Liabilities   _____

Net Worth: Assets – Liabilities   _____

Next quarterly meeting date: _____

NOTES:

ASSETS   DATE _____

    1. Cash on hand   _____

    2. Cash: Savings   _____

    3. Cash: Money Market   _____

    4. Credit Union Funds   _____

    5. Bonds   _____

    6. Stock   _____

    7. Valuable Coins   _____

    8. Other   _____

Total Assets   _____

Liabilities

    1.   _____

    2.   _____

Total Liabilities   _____

Net Worth: Assets – Liabilities   _____

Next quarterly meeting date: _____

NOTES:

ASSETS   DATE _____

    1. Cash on hand   _____

    2. Cash: Savings   _____

    3. Cash: Money Market   _____

    4. Credit Union Funds   _____

    5. Bonds   _____

    6. Stock   _____

    7. Valuable Coins   _____

    8. Other   _____

Total Assets   _____

Liabilities

    1.   _____

    2.   _____

Total Liabilities   _____

Net Worth: Assets – Liabilities   _____

Next quarterly meeting date: _____

NOTES:

Made in the USA
San Bernardino, CA
04 December 2018